SEXY MONEY

INFUSING PLEASURE AND POWER INTO MONEY WHILE YOU MAKE MORE THAN EVER

GENEVIEVE RACKHAM

Authorsunite.com

ISBNs

Paperback: 978-1-951503-59-8
Ebook: 978-1-951503-60-4

INTRODUCTION

I want to show you that you can make money and become wealthy without sacrificing your beautiful heart.

And instead create wealth in alignment with it

While moving from desire

While having fun

My desire is for you to be happy, wealthy, and turned on

And to ooze magnetism to aligned wealth from this place.

To become the fullest version of yourself and create the life you truly want, not limited by money.

When we get into alignment with what we want, clean up any fucky energy around desire, and powerfully move forward, we create a beautiful life and sexy relationship with money.

You get to feel powerful, wildly abundant and turned on, while life and money pour gasoline onto your internal fire of magic.

Money used to be an incredibly difficult concept for me. My reality around money used to be a deep source of fear, unworthiness and anxiety. As in, panic attacks, can't breathe, feeling like I'm going to die, wondering if I'd ever feel safe and supported, pain in my body, type of anxiety.

I was deeply programmed into scarcity growing up. It was a feeling of fight to survive and maybe (but probably not-muahaha) you'll sometimes have your basic needs met or disconnect from a yummy life and overcome, push until you give yourself a stress induced heart attack, pull yourself up by your bootstraps at the expense of taking really good care of yourself, spending time with those you love, and building a beautiful and meaningful life.

And... fuck all that.

If you're soul just said "FUCK YES!" You're in the right place ;)

I wanted abundance, meaning, spaciousness, to be of service, to build a beautiful life, take really good care of myself, feel elated and turned on by life and all I do and make shit tons of money.

So now my reality around money is just.. completely different.

Even during the process of writing this book, between chapters 4 and 5 my income more than doubled in a way that completely blew my mind with the level of ease, potency, and the speed at which it occurred.

As I write this book I am a 7 figure business and brand owner well on my way to creating more millions, the trajectory at which my clients and I continue to grow blows my mind. All while prioritizing taking really good care of myself honoring my spaciousness, and trusting deeply in what I desire.

Which is a far cry from where I started. Times when I was unable to meet my own basic needs, like eating. A time where my basic survival felt deeply difficult and uncertain.

With this work, I am known as an expert and this is why so many people come into my world, AND simultaneously I am always a student.

I desire this forever.

To learn continually and extend what I know, as I go, to benefit anyone who desires to learn and calibrate to it.

I will never be someone who will be a self proclaimed expert and simply choose to stop learning. I desire to honor the nature of being both an expert and a continual evolution, simultaneously.

In this, it isn't that it feels like constant striving.

It feels like a dance of honoring the growth, WHILE (not instead of) I honor what's important to me, my values, and what I stand for.

Continual evolution and… more money and continual pleasure, spaciousness, taking really good care of myself, being present in my life, creating special and intentional time with my loves ones, standing for what I believe in, and circulating my money in alignment with it all.

Throughout this book we will move swiftly and potently and get to the point. I'm going to be giving you prompts, we're going to do some foundational belief work, and bring in new ways to think about life and money. Some things will feel like a breath of fresh air, some may feel like a little spanky spank. Take what resonates and leave what doesn't.

It is my desire that as you read this book, you allow these specific codes with money and wealth creation to unlock new levels of abundance and ease around money and your experience of how you allow it into your world, how you feel spending it, and how you allow it to be a tool to deeply support you and the people and things that matter to you.

So use this book intuitively. Sit with the codes of Sexy Money inside each chapter as long as you need to and trust them to open you to more.

1

GOD AND OUR BELIEFS ABOUT GOD AND HOW IT IMPACTS WHAT WE ALLOW OURSELVES TO WANT

Saying the word God (like money) can be a little controversial

Because it can bring up all of these ideas of what we think/feel/believe about God

What we perceive other people's beliefs about who/what god is or isn't and whether other people are right and therefore we aren't, or whether we feel we are right and others are wrong and many can feel guarded and there in become defensive in looking at what they believe about God and why

For me, in the environments I was emerged in growing up

I was taught God was kind of a judgement turd

Side note- I hope you come to realize throughout this book that I have a sense of humor ;)

I hope you use it to deepen into fun and open your heart

For the longest time as a teenager I felt like I didn't believe in a God.

But what I realized was I was actually just rejecting who/what I was told about God.

That I didn't actually believe in some people's version of God. I didn't want the one size fits all, wear it even if it fits awkwardly and makes me feel like a potato. I wanted something a little more form fitting. ;)

I eventually realized my version of God didn't have to be other people's version of God

And I realized that voice within me was actually God calling me to open up to my own unique relationship with God

The fun, cool, sexy, playful, super supportive, conspiring in your favor, God.

I'm going to make a bold assumption here and say

God calls us to the relationship with (him/her/it/they/them) that we will most benefit from having in our lives through our desires.

That will allow us to not only have what we want, but also positively impact the world.

From working with so many amazing humans over the years in shifting their relationships of and to money-

God has come up, a lot.

Because a lot of the heart centered humans I work with want to have a lot of money AND be good people

And the idea of what is considered morally good and allowed has boiled down to systems and ideas that were rooted in a judgmental God with all of these rules, that if you don't follow will lead to your eternal damnation.

Like.. sounds like judgmental turd.

And not a God I can get behind.

Some people identified with these ideas consciously, some didn't even realize it was running in their internal programming until we dug deeper.

When we've dug deeper

We've noticed where these internal conflicts around being good or having money, have come from, and for many they start with our relationship to what we believe to be morally right, allowed, and acceptable and many of these stories back to our higher power and deeper belief systems around this.

Many will double down on what they were taught or reject and rebel in protest because they want to be good, acceptable, and worthy or they seek that out through rejecting what they've been taught about God in order to feel accepted or worthy and feel free in being who they are and wanting what they want

In short, They conform or reject and act accordingly.

So many people have told me I make money feel "light" which we will elaborate more on this in a later chapter.

But this stems from my relationship to God (feel free to insert whatever title you prefer) (The universe/ your higher self/ a magic magician in the sky, an all knowing lizard- or whatever)

I realized if I desired to make a lot of money and take really good care of myself while i ALSO did a lot of good in the world- I had to be willing to not feel so guilty and shitty about it and challenge and shift my ideas around God and my relationship to it.

You'll notice as we move through this book I'll be saying "AND" a lot because often we have duplicitous and conflicting ideas where we feel we have to choose and therefore we believe we have to choose between things and settle

And God told me to tell you "You're sexy, and I didn't put you here to settle- I put you here on purpose with the desires you have for a very specific reason- you are meant for greatness."

Something I often say to my clients is "God isn't a dick" meaning, God wouldn't put you here on this earth, with the desires you have and make you choose between having some at the expense of having others.

Both always gets to be the vibe.

Good person AND has lots of money

Happy AND rich

Healthy AND wealthy

Amazing relationships AND deeply satisfying career/purpose

Positively impacting others AND positively impacting self.

Happy, sexy, powerful, and wealthy.

What I've found is, when we believe in something bigger backing us and what we want we are much more available to receive it.

And when we believe that something bigger than us isn't, we aren't.

Because we're going to feel like we're being naughty (not the fun kind of naughty) for wanting in the first place.

My God beliefs are the foundation of my relationship with life, love, health, and money.

And my relationship to God is always what I lean on when doing the scary things, the next level things, and upping my ability to believe life gets to get even better.

And I believe in a God that wants us to have it all

Much like curating our relationships intentionally with others, we get to do this with our version of God- which is our relationship to life itself.

So I ask you- when you tap into your heart

What does God believe?

About who you are, what you get to have, and the life you get to live.

The God that supports your highest good, your deepest desires and the highest good of the world.

This gets to be your foundation that allows you to create a beautiful and epic life.

Feel free to journal on what you've been taught and rewrite and choose a new relationship with God

I was taught that God is: ex: a judgmental turd and I should feel guilty for wanting to be rich because wanting things is bad and not morally acceptable.

_____

_____

_____

_____

_____

_____

_____

What do I want to be true about God? ex: that God wants me to want things and to fulfill and fully receive them. That me having what I want gets to be good for me and for others. That God didn't put me here to choose between myself or others.

_____

_____

_____

_____

_____

Knowing that this is my deeper truth and guidance coming through from God, what does God actually believe? ex: God actually gives me my desires because they serve a larger purpose that I don't always need to understand. That they are my guidance for my blueprint in this life. That I'm here to not just live but have some fun with the earth stuff.

2

WHO ARE YOU AND WHAT RELATIONSHIP DO YOU DESIRE TO HAVE WITH MONEY?

There so many icky and limiting ideas floating around about money.

And these ideas keep good people separated from money

And when we do this- who ends up with money?

Not the good people who will do good shit with it.

These ideas include but aren't limited to:

Rich people are selfish and greedy

If they're rich they must be fucking someone else over for it.

Being rich OR having deeply satisfying love

Being wealthy OR being healthy

Being a good person and helping people OR being rich

Freedom and Spaciousness OR getting and being rich

The list goes on

And quite frankly

These ideas are limiting, boring, and completely optional.

Sure, these versions of life exist and some people throughout history have done some not so great things when acquiring wealth and have showed that these ideas are possible.

But I want to highlight something important to you: they're possible, but fully optional

And these ideas don't have to mean anything about you and what you get to have.

You are you

And you get to lead by example

And create a new path that is completely yours.

When desiring to admit, that you as someone who desires to be a good person, also desires to be wealthy as fuck

You have to know who you are

And more so what I mean by that is, you get to decide who you are.

Because money doesn't have the power to change you, it can only amplify who you already are.

You get to create yourself and your reality intentionally.

And Act and live in alignment with that

So...

Who are you?

What do you want?

And who do you WANT to be and therefore dedicate yourself to be while you allow yourself to receive what you want?

And when it comes to money, just like God- we get to create our own unique relationship to it and experience of it, a unique blueprint that support us.

It's also important to know who you choose to be because as you are someone who is brave enough to pursue the desires of your heart- you may experience people trying to tell you who you are, what you should do, who you should be, and how you should live your life based on their own fears, doubts, and insecurities.

And one who doesn't have a solid inner world, will often allow others people perception of them and what they think about what we want, to dictate who we become and how we live our lives.

And that's not who we came here to be.

You did not come here to play small or to shrink in the face of your desires or in the presence of others.

We came here to be who we want to be.

When you drop the guilt, shame, and unnecessary sacrifice around money..

When money doesn't have to be a source of evil, pain, heaviness, etc.

When money can be viewed as a neutral resource and tool that can be used for good by good people AND you can take really good care of yourself and have a beautiful, comfortable, and fun life, money will match us.

Who do you desire to be in the world with money? Don't censor or filter what comes through. Allow it. For many, they haven't even allowed themselves to go there. And it's time.

_____

_____

_____

_____

_____

How do you want your relationship with money to be?

_____

_____

_____

_____

_____

These are all on going things we get to continually change and upgrade.

For me it's-

I take really good care of myself with my money AND I do good in the world with my money

I make a lot of money AND nourish myself and honor my spaciousness

God wouldn't give me the desires I have if they weren't meant for me- my job is to get willing, receptive, and cooperative to my desires.

I do good in the world AND receive massively

Money doesn't take me away from what I desire, I make money as an extension of following that which I desire fully and completely.

As I allow myself to receive without guilt and shame I give others permission to do the same.

Sure I may piss people off too because money can be loaded topic for many.

I used to be the person who thought money was evil

That it was always a struggle

That there was never enough

That rich people were greedy

That it wasn't for people "like me"

When people would talk about money, I would cringe and get really uncomfortable.

Then I realized, if I can't even talk about money and my desire is to have a lot of it, I have work to do.

When anyone would appear to have a lot of it, I would judge them and assume things about their life or character.

And on a deeper level then that, that I probably wouldn't admit easily at the time ;)

I wondered why other people had it and I didn't.

Why it seemed to come so naturally to some people and felt like pulling teeth or a struggle to survive to others. (Like me)

And I'm aware this is the case for many people still.

It takes a certain level of willingness to shift these ideas and begin having a different experience and relationship to money and life itself.

It wasn't until I began challenging these ideas about money that I could then see, feel, and experience money differently.

As I talk about money, or anything throughout this book for that matter, I invite you to notice what comes up for you and be willing to examine and question it.

Some things may make you feel lighter.

Some things may piss you off and make you want to throw this book at a wall.

It's all allowed, but it's what we do with it that matters.

The first and most powerful step to changing anything is noticing the current programs that are playing out for us and getting curious about what else could be available.

And then challenging these ideas.

Where did these limiting ideas with money come from? Do they have to be true for YOU? No.

You can either use examples of those who have gone before and created similar to what you desire or you can lead and be the first.

When you're willing to get curious about where your limiting ideas come from, you can see that they were not the ultimate truth or your destiny.

Your desires can lead you instead of your past programming.

So we get to look at-

What do you actually believe about money?

_____

_____

_____

_____

_____

_____

Where did you learn this? Where did these ideas come from?

_____

_____

_____

_____

_____

Do they have to be your truth?

_____

_____

_____

_____

_____

What ideas, beliefs, and feelings do you need to let go of in order to have the life with money you want?

_____

_____

_____

_____

_____

_____

What would you have to believe in order to create the relationship with life and money you want?

_____

_____

_____

_____

_____

_____

I had a lot of issues around money, where I felt unworthy and all the things you could probably think of.

But my biggest hang up around money- What I have referred to as my deepest wounding around money, to my clients, in the beginning of me doing this work, was scarcity. And from here I lived in hella lack.

I felt the lack and also experienced the lack in my life.

The feeling of not having enough and never having enough.

The feeling of money being extremely limited in general and especially to me.

It wasn't just a thought in my head, or something I believed to be true, or even just a real experience for me, it was deeply ingrained in my body.

It was a full physical response I had to money.

I would think about money and my body would take over with fear and panic.

Where my body felt deeply unsafe.

And I spiraled to the point of feeling like I could't breathe, like everything was spinning, and I felt like I was going to die.

I later found out that these experiences were panic attacks.

10/10 wouldn't recommend, not fun. Hehe

It took real work and healing to train myself out of that response

And to eventually train myself into feeling and believing new things about money

And eventually into having a completely different experience with money.

But I had to be willing to trust that the desires of my heart were God given.

That they were meant to be.

That they were good.

That they were for me.

They they were destined.

And I had to make the loudest voice in my world my internal voice

Louder than the people around me

Louder than the my own fears, doubts, and insecurities.

The loudest voice of all.

And I had to make my most real vision, the one I saw inside of myself

More real than what I had always thought, felt, and believed about myself, life, money and what I could have.

More real than my past experiences

More real than what I saw around me

More real than what others told me and showed me

I had to do this without absolutely any evidence in my external world to validate my internal vision

And do this without needing any support from those around me, who many were well meaning and some weren't.

I had to decide who I was anyways

Who I would be either way

And what I would have and create regardless

Not everyone will get it, and that's okay.

Whether that's family, friends, neighbors, strangers on the internet, it doesn't matter.

Some people don't know how to and that's okay.

Some people don't want to for their own conscious or unconscious reasons, and that's okay.

You are more powerful than letting any of that stop you or slow you down.

You don't need the approval, you don't need the understanding, you don't need the applause.

Even if you're the only mother fucking person in your life who believes in you.

We have to clap for ourselves first, usually people come around, and some may not, but we can't need them to in order to create the life we want.

You are here to lead. You are here to lead yourself, inspire and potentially piss off and awaken anyone who needs it by you fiercely following the desires of your heart.

If you following the desires of your heart bothers anyone, let it.

I believe we were given free will for a reason, we can let other people, past experiences, and life tell us who we are or we can choose who we are.

So let me ask you again, who do you want to be?

This is ACTUALLY the truth of who you are at your core.

We just have to open to it.

Welcome to the mother fucking awakening. ;)

You didn't pick up this book by accident, you're here for more.

Who are you? How will life meet you? The desires of your heart are already who you are, you just have to be brave enough to own them now.

Yes, right now.

Then life will greet you accordingly.

Something I had to remind myself of, was I am the leading energy in my life.

If I'm willing to hold the energy within myself powerfully and with conviction

The world, money, and other people must get on my frequency and respond to me accordingly.

Things will have to move

Mountains would move if needed

Things would change

Things would work

Life would shift.

And over time it did.

I am _____ I live _____ kind of life.

Money loves me. I am wealthy. I live a beautiful life.

The end.

3

LIGHT MONEY AND HEALING THE FEELING OF SCARCITY

I want you to know that money can feel light

That you can feel safe with money that you can trust yourself with money

And that the tight feeling of scarcity gets to shift.

After healing myself of this feeling

And helping many others do the same over the years

There's been a common theme on this subject of scarcity.

Wanting to feel safe with money

Wanting to trust that you'll be supported by money

Wanting things to work out instead of getting the shitty end of the stick and it always feeling like a struggle or it feeling hard.

Money can be a friend and an ally instead of a necessary evil that you have to tolerate and deal with.

Money can be a beautiful tool in your life instead of a bully.

It is to safe to be incredibly wealthy. You can trust yourself, you can handle it.

And if you don't want money, cool! Get rich and give it to other people.

When I broke down the feeling of "Not enough money and never enough money"

I realized it boiled down to wanting to feel safe.

FEELING safe with money

I'm repeating myself with emphasis on purpose.

Something I had to realize around healing scarcity with money was I was always just looking for a different feeling.

I was wanting to feel safe, free, and worthy of more.

And I was making that money's responsibility

And giving my power away to money.

And therefore was never actually free when it came to money.

I jokingly say "I was money's bitch."

It had ultimate power over me, how I felt, the decisions I made, how I felt about myself, and how I felt about life.

My experience of it dictated how I felt and lived my life.

What I had to realize was money was and never will be the source of whether or not I feel a certain type of way unless I allow it to be.

At first in order to heal myself of the scarcity patterning, it had to stop being the source of whether I felt safe and secure or not.

Sure it came from very real experiences of mine with money and life.

Past memories and times when I didn't have money to eat which brings up a very primal survival response.

It doesn't mean what you've experienced up until this point wasn't real or is't valid.

It means you're willing to heal from the past and move forward into something new.

A new feeling response to, and relationship with money.

When I could learn to separate that feeling response from money, I could identify it more as an emotional issue that required healing instead of needing to change anything in my experience of money in order to feel safe and better.

Because if I always needed money to change in order to feel better I would never be truly free or happy.

And I wouldn't be leading my life, I would be letting life and ultimately my past lead me.

From there, I wouldn't be on the frequency of having more.

And what I wanted more than anything was not just to fulfill my desires but to be truly happy and fulfilled and build my vision on top of that.

What I began to realize was this feeling of scarcity was trying to keep me stuck in a loop of repeating the same things over and over again.

That my brain was latching onto what was familiar and therefore felt safe on a deeper level.

And that by repeating this pattern again and again was actually my minds way of trying to keep me safe.

Because after all, this pattern never killed me, it just kept me in struggle and that was safe, comfortable, and controllable pattern for me on a subconscious level.

When I started looking at my brain as a really old survival mechanism I realized my thoughts and my own mind didn't always have my own best interest in mind.

And if I kept repeating the same pattern- I would never breakthrough and thrive, I would simply stay stuck in a cycle of survival.

I noticed this because I began to pay attention to my mind with this pattern and I saw that it would begin "predicting my future"

We will often "predict our future" when we are activated by something that takes us out of the present moment, make it the ultimate truth (even when it isn't) and make decisions in alignment with it.

For example: "If you spend this money, you're going to run out."

So many just won't spend it or invest it, or do it and activate their deeper fears that can be and get to be cleared and shifted.

When I followed that train of thought of "If you spend this money, you're going to run out." I realized my brain was afraid of dying.

"If you spend this money, this will lead to running out. You'll never have more or make more. Then you're not going to be able to pay your bills. Then you're going to be homeless. Then you're going to not be able to eat. Then you're going to die."

It was completely illogical to feel like I would never make more because money can replenish, but it felt true that it wouldn't because my nervous system was attached to the moment of money flowing out and making it an ever lasting eternity.

My brain was getting out ahead of me and my current experience constantly and always predicting the worst case scenario and my "failure"

So naturally I felt, acted, and created in alignment with it.

Over and over again until I was sick of it.

The feeling response I had to that pattern made it feel very real even if it wasn't yet, or wasn't actually ever going to be.

And one day I noticed it and said "Does this have to be true? Does this have to keep being the pattern?"

And I consciously chose the response "ew NO!"

If I was willing to explore that more was possible for me, I had to be willing to explore the fact that this pattern could end, and therefore end up being wrong.

From there I began questioning everything I thought and felt that wasn't in alignment with the life I wanted, including my experience of money.

I began this process that I later coined as "pulling the thread"

I explain this process to my clients like this..

When I was a kid and my necklaces in my jewelry box would get tangled and there was a specific one I wanted to wear, like my favorite "G" necklace I got from the mall, I had to pull on it to start the process of un-tanglement.

Sometimes just pulling on it would naturally untangle the knot

Other times it would untangle slightly then get stuck again and require more pulling closer to the root of the knot.

I'm sure we've all experienced this with our shoe laces at some point, right? Hehe

As we are willing to continue to move forward towards all that we desire, whether we feel safe to, worthy of it, or ready for it, or not.

And we move anyways because we choose to.

We begin to bring to the surface the things that we feel, believe, practice and have held on to that are in the way of us settling naturally into our new and desired experiences.

As these things come to the surface we need to process and shift them in order to release them and create a new version of ourselves, which is made up of what we feel think, believe and expect.

Let's break down my process for pulling the thread.

You notice an uncomfortable feeling has surfaced because you're challenging yourself, you're doing something growth oriented, or a life experience has simply nudged it out of you, or its randomly just popping up and it's either subtle or intense or somewhere in between.

You take deep breaths and identify where you feel it in your body

You place your hands lovingly over the area to connect deeper with this feeling

You ask yourself, "What am I feeling?"

I'll use my past feelings of scarcity as an example.

(This is just one example and you can sometimes feel it in multiple areas at once or once in one place then it resurfaces in another area- you simply use this process again and again as needed)

"I feel it in my chest"

I placed my hands over my heart

I then ask myself "What am I feeling and why?"

"I'm afraid."

Why?

"Because I don't feel safe."

Why?

"Because I don't have money/ Or I don't have enough money"

What are you making that mean?

"That I'm not going to be okay. That I will never have more and I won't be able to eat. That I will become homeless. That I will suffer and die."

There it is.

This is the root of "the knot"

Sometimes just identifying it clears it immediately because we realize the connection we've made is silly and not true.

Spending money = dying

Dramatic, right?

When we feel it as tension in our body- it needs to be expressed to move out.

Often this looks like moving our bodies.

Going for a run, dancing, etc.

This movement moves the energy up and out.

I would hold my hands over my chest and say "I love you- it's okay that you feel this way. And you are safe right now. In this moment you are safe."

If we judge ourselves for what we're feeling we can't move past them.

If we judge ourselves for what we're feeling we end up compounding other emotions on top of them, which just adds another layer on top of it.

And the thing with feelings is, they aren't always the truth in the moment

Sometimes they're a memory that's stored in our bodies that want to be processed and released.

If any specific memory surfaces, I invite you to hold space for the younger or past version of you and give yourself a lot of love and see what inspired action comes through for you to process.

Maybe its a conversation you have with yourself, maybe it's a letter you write to someone from your past where you let it all out and don't send it (or send it, if it feels aligned for you.)

Maybe you just need to cry or beat up your pillows.

Maybe it's just to acknowledge it and allow it to release naturally.

But let it out and let it move.

This is how you move past it.

You can do the exercise of pulling the thread here:

You ask yourself, "What am I feeling?"

_____

_____

_____

_____

_____

_____

Why?

_____

_____

_____

_____

_____

Why?

_____

_____

_____

_____

_____

_____

What are you making that mean?

_____

_____

_____

_____

_____

_____

What am I feeling led to do to process and release this limiting idea? Knowing that it isn't true or doesn't have to be true.

_____

_____

_____

_____

_____

_____

Then go do it ;)

Sometimes you just need to feel and acknowledge it and it moves out of you.

Sometimes you don't feel it in your body and it's just a thought pattern.

Meaning, the only place you feel it is actively in your mind as an internal narrative.

From here we get to get curious and question it, challenge it, and then decide what we want to be true for us and our life experience instead and practice this in it's place.

Then we begin acting thinking and practicing in alignment with this new chosen belief, instead of the ones we absorbed unconsciously through our past experiences.

And through repetition we can shift into believing something new.

The thing with scarcity is, we put our sense of safety, wellbeing, and ability to feel good and we attach it to our dollars (or lack there of)

We go "Oh I don't have a lot of money in the bank" and then we make it mean something and/or we predict the future with it, which isn't fair because the future is malleable and isn't for sure yet.

We make it mean something is going to happen and play out a certain way.

We make it mean that we aren't going to be okay

That we aren't going to be able to do what we want.

And we respond to our money.

Which is very logical, and there in feels reasonable to us and is acceptable in our society.

But in logic we fall into what's logical for us, not necessarily what's actually true, going to be true, or can be true.

We do this based on what we've been taught and what we've already experienced and we re-create the same patterns over and over again.

"When we change the way we look at things, the things we look at change." -Wayne Dyer

Another way to say this is, when we begin to feel differently about our circumstances, our circumstances begin to change.

If we are unable to expand past our logic because we don't trust that it could be different and play in a new feeling experience, we are unable to explore a different version of reality, with different outcomes available to us.

And therefore we are less available to experience it because we are less open to it.

I'm sure you've had a moment where a situation played out differently than you expected.

Better than expected.

I'll tell you one of mine.

I started doing work on my relationship with money- the evidence that it was working was pretty slim to none at that point and mostly the only difference I experienced was in how I felt about money, I was feeling lighter.

I was living with my mom and my saving grace became being able to make it to Starbucks and buy myself an iced coffee.

Somehow some way, most days I would get an iced coffee.

Whether someone bought it for me, or I somehow acquired a few dollars.

It happened.

One day, I pulled into Starbucks, my gas light was on- I didn't have money except for some change I had in my car which I knew was enough to get an iced coffee

I ordered my coffee in the first part of the drive through and pulled ahead.

I had 2 cars in front of me and now, one behind me.

I was blocked in.

I was working on getting into a grateful state for the day and actively working on changing how I felt even though there was no evidence yet, I was practicing sourcing this feeling from myself. I was feeling solid for the most part and reached in the side compartment of my car for the change.

And it wasn't there.

Immediately I filled with embarrassment, shame, guilt, frustration, and a feeling of defeat.

As the car in front of me pulled away, and I was trying to hold back tears, as I had just had a conversation with myself where I decided to just tell them the truth "I thought I had the money, and I don't, I'm so so sorry."

As I opened my mouth to speak, the barista interrupted me and said "The car in front of you paid for your coffee! Have a nice day!"

I thanked him, pulled into a parking space and sobbed.

And I held onto this moment.

The little moments when I had evidence.

I leaned on moments like this to increase my faith again and again as I intentionally redirected my sense of safety into trusting God and the Universe.

And I started making money and more money and more money and more money.

If we want to be free of Scarcity not only in feeling but also in circumstance,

We have to stop attaching our emotional wellbeing to money.

Regardless of what's in or not in our bank accounts.

We have to make it about something else.

Something bigger.

For me, my sense of safety comes from my inner world and my connection to being supported by God and The Universe. I lean on these beliefs as the foundation.

I know it's always there and I can always tune in and feel that.

The thing is we get to find a place within ourselves where we always feel safe and stable regardless of the outwards conditions of our lives.

It doesn't mean we will always find it in every moment, but it means we know that its always available.

The interesting thing with our minds is, when that sensation of not feeling safe with money comes up, your mind is racing into the future of worst case scenarios, and your body responds, because you're mind can't really tell the difference between an imagined or real immediate threat.

But when we can ground and come back into our bodies, realize that we are actually safe and okay in that moment, we can start programming ourselves differently.

When I began programming my sense of safety in myself, I would feel the panic, close my eyes, and breathe.

I knew that the sensation happening in my body was a fear response from my mind, that was ultimately boiling down to a fear of dying.

I would breathe deeply and intentionally and touch my chest, feel my skin, get really present and say "Here I still am."

Over and over.

I was essentially talking to my mind and body and saying "LOOK I'M ALIVE!"

Nothing is hurting me or killing me.

Here I still am. Here I still am. Here I still am.

Over time, my mind and body began to realize there wasn't actually a fear of dying associated with money, so I stopped needing it to perform for me to feel safe and okay, and from here could begin playing with and holding the energy for what I actually wanted.

I could create in alignment with it, see clearly and not from lack.

I could then be fully present with my experience of money from a less emotional place and I could be more intentional.

I could spend and invest money without my sense of wellbeing leaving with the dollars.

I could make decisions based on what I wanted and process my emotions, and choose what I wanted to believe instead.

Instead of make decisions (or lack there of) based on my fears, doubts, and insecurities.

Then I started making decisions based on what I wanted instead of what I had in the moment and fear of loss.

When we're afraid of losing, we consciously and/or unconsciously do everything we can to preserve what we have instead of actively feeling and doing things differently which can create circumstances where we thrive.

If we desire to thrive we have to be willing to entertain the voice within us that believes we can.

And swiftly and continually act, feel, and believe in alignment with that.

4

DUALITY AND TRANSMUTING OUR SHIT

Sometimes your deepest desires will live in the same house as some of your deepest fears.

Walking with this duality and moving towards what we want is required in order to have our deepest desires met.

We can move toward having what we want and feeling excited while simultaneously feeling scared we aren't "enough"

Walking in the world of potentiality of what if it works and what if it doesn't will both always exist and both always be options.

This is the nature of living a dualistic existence.

But the what if it doesn't, doesn't have to be the outcome.

When we're willing to move toward what we want in the times where we feel powerful and confident (we're on the side of the coin of "what if it works?")

And also move towards it when we have fear and doubt (this is when we're on the side of the coin where we're playing with "what if it doesn't?")

We can be met with what we want

As long as we keep moving toward it

Sometimes it's effortless and sexy

Sometimes it's racing heart, sweaty palms, vomit on our sweaters already, moms spaghetti. (what's up Eminem)

And still we get to move

I deeply believe we get to feel good.

But that doesn't mean we get to opt out of this human thing and it's fullest experience, which is dualistic.

We have to learn to walk with it.

Knowing we will be okay.

We can handle it.

And we get to break through to the better feelings and better experiences.

Often, a hell of a lot faster when we're willing to hold the duality and keep moving anyways.

Our thoughts and feelings are sometimes just things moving through us- instead of real truths

Sometimes they're a voice from someone we've heard and internalized.

Sometimes they're assumptions we've made based on our experiences.

But none of them have to own us or dictate what we do or create.

When I first started my business and began investing in mentorship

I practiced and grew the muscle with the side of the coin that says "but what if it works?"

I did things with my money, that people in my life told me was not practical or "responsible"

Some were SUPER well meaning and came from deep love, *ahem* "Hi dad!"

And some weren't but either way I decided that to me, the most practical and responsible thing was for me to move towards what I wanted to create and learn to handle any potential fear, doubt, and anxiety that would come up along the way.

In order to attract something we have to be able to hold it in its full experience of duality and know that we can handle it, or wait until we clear out the fear so what's left is the good feelings where we feel good about having it, then we allow it.

This is often where we can block having what we want unconsciously, Because some part of us doesn't feel we can handle having it or keeping it. But actually we can.

Most people don't realize this is going on until they're given pieces of what they desire and then feel tight and contracted and even a little "tested."

Which is actually just the universe offering it to us when enough of our resistance has subsided and us seeing if we feel we can "handle it" or hold it.

We want to make it the new normal standard for our lives and it's giving us the opportunity to lean into full receiving and holding of it.

So we must strengthen anything around holding it that makes us wobble or waver.

When we are bold enough to move towards that which we desire

Life gives us the opportunity to clear what is keeping us energetically apart from it

So we can feel energetically clean in holding it

So when we receive it we can easily keep it

Then we do

This takes courage.

Because it isn't always immediate

Sometimes we shift pretty fast

Sometimes it takes us a minute to see it

This is why support is valuable

But for those who are willing to keep moving towards it anyways- detached from "when."

Those are the ones who clean up the duplicitous energies faster and can hold it sooner.

If we wait to move towards it- we aren't presented with the same opportunities by life

Because life isn't clear if we actually want it or not.

Because we aren't moving towards it.

When we are courageous enough to lead our lives, life will respond.

One of my favorite examples of holding it on both ends is, think about having 10 times the amount of money you do now. Really take a moment to connect to it and feel it.

Maybe you notice you feel some tension and anxiety because the idea of it freaks you out.

Now let's feel into why it freaks you out.

We have to clean up this freak out energy.

Because imagine having more of what you want?

It would sit on top of this and that would feel REALLY uncomfortable.

And our egos LOVE to avoid what's uncomfortable because it associates bad feelings with something bad happening and that tends to not feel so safe to move toward.

And this is where our innate desire to survive kicks in and keeps us playing a lot smaller than we ultimately desire.

This is often why people can tend to stay within a zone of reality that feels familiar because it feels safer, even if it actually isn't better.

When I was in my cycle of scarcity with money, I realized it actually did feel safer on a deeper level to me, and that's why it felt better on a deeper level to stay there.

So I did.

Until I didn't.

Because when my survival based part of my brain looked at the facts.

The facts were that I was still alive and breathing and "safe" within this cycle of not having enough.

Even if that meant not thriving.

To the unconscious, survival is a better bet than the "risk" of thriving.

Now that you have context, let's take it a little deeper.

Imagine someone who feels a subtle unconscious fear of running out of money.

That will feel easier to navigate with less money.

That way there is "less to lose."

Often times we don't allow what we truly want because we have these ideas of what it'll require of us that feel either unsafe, icky, not in alignment with our values, or some of these or all of these. And it isn't until we shift these that we can experience a deeper ease with money.

The deeper ease is a byproduct of us no longer having a push/pull thing going on with what we want.

So it flows in easier.

Maybe the idea of having a lot more money feels like a lot of responsibility and that scares you and makes you feel trapped.

With this idea your only option is to push it away or suck it up and feel like poop in your experience of money.

Most people will simply, unconsciously, choose to push it away.

Because they don't want to experience the uncomfortable feelings they've programmed themselves to believe are associated with what they want.

Those who simply choose to suck it up and push through with the internal resistance going on, earn a lot less and it feels a lot harder than it has to be.

Maybe you fear that if you were to allow in so much money, you wouldn't be able to sustain it and maybe even lose it all because that experience of money "isn't for you."

Maybe you fear that people would judge you or even hurt you.

We get to take a look at these things and change these.

But first we must realize it's going on underneath the surface.

Maybe the idea of it feels sexy, solid, and delicious.

This is what we want.

But if the idea of being someone who operates at that level, spends at a level that's equivalent in your mind, scares you and activate feelings of loss, then we have some work to do.

Because for some, it's one thing to have millions but to be someone who's circulating millions can feel like a lot of potential loss or responsibility.

This is what I mean by holding it on both ends.

Does the desire feeeeeeel good, safe, and solid and does being the person who operates at this level also feel good, safe, and solid?

If not, we need to address what makes it feel unsafe and trust that you can handle it.

The thing that makes you feel unsafe are the things that feel bad, creepy, and/or undesirable, as a "what if."

When we're willing to look at the things we're afraid of underneath the surface and realize that we can handle it, we can then alchemize it.

From here it's no longer active within us or a driving force of our life experiences.

A few years ago, after I made $24,000.00 in 1 month, I activated a deeper fear.

I didn't know anyone in my personal, real, life who made this much money.

It was the sexy "multiple 6 figure level in business"

But deeper down, 6 figures felt safer, more under the radar.

A level of income I knew that some people did and was considered somewhat normal and acceptable to some people.

I felt panic arise in my body.

I leaned into it and it stemmed back to a deeper fear of someone taking it from me, manipulating me, or physically hurting me to acquire it.

This was based on real past experiences.

Feeling as though I had to give someone money who felt entitled to it, wanted it, or demanded it who I knew had the capacity to hurt me because they had before.

The next month I made less, because unconsciously it felt safer.

It wasn't until I cleared this fear out of my system that I was then able to not only sustain it but long surpass that milestone.

I asked myself "Okay brain, what are you afraid of?"

It said, "Someone's going to demand it from me."

My inner power said- "We can say no because, yay healthy boundaries."

My brain- "What if they and take it anyways and hurt me to take it?"

Inner power- "We can stop them or let it go and just make more."

My brain- "What if they kill me for it?"

Inner power- "Well then we'd be dead and it would be over and what would there be to worry about then?"

Some may think that's a little dark but I personally found it funny and helpful.

I felt a shift.

A calm.

A feeling of knowing it was pretty irrational BUT if any of my fears happened I had the capacity to handle it and/or I just stopped feeling attached to those fears and released the charge around it.

I could feel safe to allow myself to make and receive more.

By doing that, there was no longer a big charge I felt I had to resist, which is where the resistance and push pull comes in.

And I allowed more in.

Sometimes when you feel into the things under the surface, they will feel irrational or very justifiable.

And either way, we get to release it.

Because what I know about this work, from doing it myself, and mentoring many others to do the same is, we are far more capable and powerful than we sometimes realize.

And sometimes we don't know it until we check in with ourselves or experience what we're afraid of and rise to the challenge.

Once we address these ideas and begin feeling powerful enough to hold it all in alignment with our values and priorities, we tend to feel a lot more comfortable receiving it and then allow ourselves to call it in.

Another piece of the duality conversation is when we can hold the flip side we can easily call in what we actually want because there is no charge around fear of the flip side of it.

For example, recently one of my clients in my high level mastermind (The Sexy Wealthy Bitch mastermind) asked me something powerful.

She said, "I notice when new people come into the space they automatically calibrate to how you run the container without you explaining it to them."

She asked why and how this is the case because we wanted to have this experience inside her high level containers.

I said, "Because I'm not afraid of the flip side."

Meaning, I'm not afraid of someone purposely or accidentally crossing my boundaries because I know I could handle it and clean it up easily.

It would cause me zero anxiety. I wouldn't lose any sleep over it.

I would just address it with ease and move on.

Because of this, I don't attract it.

Because I don't have a "charge" around it and therefore no level of magnetizing it into my experience.

For that reason, it's just not a part of my experience anymore.

I developed this level of power and certainty around it because I had situations where I had to handle it and deal with it and now I know deeply, that I can handle it.

It doesn't mean we have to experience the duality in order to easily hold space for what we actually want.

It just means we have to feel solid and know we can handle it so we no longer hold a charge around it and can easily, and without resistance hold space for and call in what we actually want.

Another example, I used to be afraid of clients leaving my world.

And so I would block even more of them coming in.

Because I couldn't energetically and emotionally "handle" them potentially leaving.

Because of this I would only allow in the amount of people I could "handle" leaving/if they left.

So this blocked my ability to hold space for more people.

I would get really attached to them. I would fall in love with their journey and who they are and their growth and would get really sad if they left because they felt complete and it was aligned.

This was the block.

It wasn't until I shifted this, that I could then hold space for more and more aligned clients to come into my world. Or as I call them, soul aligned, fuck yes clients.

(I define the soul aligned fuck yes clients as the clients who are a perfect energetic match to coming into our world right now.)

When I was okay with people leaving when it was their aligned time and I could still love them and honor their journey and not feel bad about it anymore, more people began coming into my world.

Because what I realized is, some people aren't supposed to be in my world for a long time and that's okay.

Some are only aligned with the minimum time, some a little longer, some that want to stay indefinitely.

I could still love them all, honor them all, and feel solid, either way.

From here, I could hold it all and there in stop protecting myself from the flip side, and from there call in what I actually wanted.

I would love for you to feel into this for yourself and see if anything needs to be cleaned up.

What do you want?

_____

_____

_____

_____

_____

What is the flip side of what you want? AKA the "what if"

_____

_____

_____

_____

_____

Do you feel solid and energetically neutral in the experience of the flip side? or not?

_____

_____

_____

_____

_____

There is no wrong answer, there is just awareness.

From here, life will always help you get ready, this is when we start attracting situations that make us feel "tested" like I mentioned previously in this chapter. But actually it's life being a loyal and devout lover and supporter.

When we can create awareness around the flip side of the coin sooner, and clear it intentionally we won't unconsciously create experiences that make us feel "tested."

Can you actually not handle the "what if" "worst case scenario?" Or is it that you would maybe just be scared and end up being okay and move on with your life?

Another way to dig into this is we can sometimes unconsciously block what we want, when we have different parts of ourselves working against each other because part of us wants it and part of us doesn't, and this is why it can feel hard.

When we can become aware of what part of us doesn't actually want it, because we believe having it will take more than it gives, see if it's actually a real concern or not, and shift it, we can cleanly receive it.

I like to explain it like.. imagine you're a kid laying in bed at night in what is, a mostly dark room. Your closet door is slightly ajar and you think you see something in the closet.

You convince yourself there is a monster in there.

The longer you stare at it, the bigger it gets, the harder it is to get out of bed.

If you were to just get out of bed and go look, you would find out the truth.

But if we're not willing to look, we don't move.

As this applies to life and money, we don't allow movement in our lives and flow of dollars.

So one of two things occurs, you get up and look in the closet and see it was just one of your coats, there was never anything there.

Or.. there really is a monster in there.

But at least now you know what you're dealing with, and can deal with it accordingly.

I talk about this a lot with money and business.

One of the ways I teach on it is in relationship to bringing clients into your world, sometimes people want to consciously but also don't more unconsciously.

An easy example is, you want more clients from a really clean and pure place, you love serving people, you feel solid with your prices, all the things.

BUT you feel a little overwhelmed in your life, you don't really feel like you have a lot of time.

The thing is, clients WILL require your time. Mind blowing, I know. ;)

So you block clients because they would take more of your time, even if this isn't a conscious realization you've had.

So I would sit down and look, are you actually busy? Or are you just "feeling" busy?

Do you actually not have time for them or do you just feel like you don't have time for them?

Yes there is a difference.

If you "feel" like you don't have time, when you actually sit and look at your schedule and your day to day life, you'll see you actually do have time. The monster was just a coat and you can relax and be open and available to more powerful people coming into your world.

Or you'll see that there is indeed a monster and you don't actually have the amount of time that feels good to take on more clients.

Time to make some choices of working with people differently, move things around, or evolve how you work with your clients so you can still show up powerfully for them but with less of your time.

Yes, it can be done.

Journal on what part of me doesn't want what I want?

Step 1- What do you want?

_____

_____

_____

_____

Step 2- Is there any reason, any part of you wouldn't want it? Why?

_____

_____

_____

_____

_____

Step 3- What do I need to look at and clear in order to shift this?

_____

_____

_____

_____

_____

5

DESIRE

Desire is a frequency of pure attraction and magnetism in the universe

It's an energy we have to learn to calibrate to and understand

What I mean by this is, we have to learn how to know what we truly actually want and lead from this energy because this is where life (and money) will crack open for you.

When we do we tend to stay in the energy of cleanly wanting (not lacking)

The issue with this is it's an energy that not a lot of people are acclimated to.

Often when they think about wanting something, they're really actually thinking about not having something they want.

From this energy you'll notice a contraction in your body, however subtle or obvious.

The contraction feels like a tightening and closing off

Because that's exactly what it is

It's closing off to that inherent inner power of attraction

And it's a closing off to a deeper experience of life.

But when we learn how to want things from an energy of pure and clean desire, we feel excited and in my own experience, turned on.

The cool thing about this is, it won't just make you a lot more money, it will you up to life on a deeper level, altogether.

The thing is..

A lot of people are programmed to be disconnected from this inherent and inner voice of pleasure and desire.

This shows up as "not knowing what you want."

Guilt and shame about what you want

Thinking you want things you actually don't right now

And all of this takes us off track of creating a pleasurable life and experience of money.

One who is trained and acclimated to their inner voice of desire is a force to be reckoned with in the world.

Their the ones who life just seems to open up to.

I want you to become this person.

Desire is something we have to dance with to become more and more familiar with its specific frequency

And it's not a box we check it's a continual dance we participate in daily that acclimates us to living in it and from it.

Because like I said, when we live here- money flows, we meet the partner, the opportunity appears, etc.

Life just opens to us.

In order to acclimate to this voice, we have to unpack what keeping us in touch with it, inherently.

I believe, owning this energy is inherent on our deepest level.

We just have to clean up what's sitting on top of it so we can feel it.

First we have to know what we want.

This can be an elusive feeling process for many. Because this is where the inner ego typically steps up to the plate instead of the inherent voice of desire.

And the thing with this is, it's standing in the way of the deeper voice.

And people will build a life led by this voice instead of desire, and never quite feel fulfilled, happy, or fully alive.

They'll chase what they think they will make them feel better or settle often into mediocrity, simply because they can't feel and hear this voice.

Essential they're living a life that feels a little dull.

The voices that show up and cock block this inherent connectedness will often show up at the "inner control freak"

The inner "I don't know what I want's"

The inner "Who the fuck do I think I am's"

And when we unpack these things and see them for what they are, we can begin sorting through the internal static and begin fine tuning to the clarity of our desires.

The word desire in and of itself for some people can be a loaded topic.

There can be this association that it's naughty or inherently bad or wrong or not allowed.

I see this show up in a lot of people who say they don't consciously believe this but still do unconsciously.

This shows up in their thoughts and lives.

The thing is, that voice isn't yelling in your head "desire is bad!" Or maybe it is for some of you.

And if it is, you get to get curious about this thought, challenge it and be open to something else.

Ultimately you have to ask yourself, do I WANT this to be true?

And if the answer is no, then it isn't and doesn't have to be for you.

For many who don't consciously identify with this belief but still have it going on up there somewhere, it's often that feeling of guilt.

That if you could ask it if it could talk, which I recommended,

It would be saying something like "me having means it's taking from someone else"

Or "I'm not allowed to have that"

Or whatever notion that is convincing for you.

Because your brain knows you, it's going to pull on every idea that feels true to you, pull convincing evidence that it is INDEED true and you're a terrible turd, of a person.

It's job is to reinforce what you believe to be true.

So if we don't question these ideas we will walk around with whatever limiting ideas that have been imprinted on us and call it fate.

Or say "that's just life."

Let's start with shame.

When we feel guilty for wanting a good life because we have deeper ideas about it being naughty or taking from other people

ahem hey sneaky ego.

Our ego will try and protect us from knowing what we actually want.

I've seen this time and time again, with myself and many of my clients over the years.

Often it isn't actually that we don't know, it's that we don't consciously know because we don't feel comfortable admitting it, unconsciously.

So we suppress our knowingness.

First, we have to acknowledge and even own the fact, that wanting is good.

Desire is what moves ourselves, our lives, and the collective world forward.

Without it, we wouldn't move.

It's an inherent piece of people.

To want, makes us move.

Movement creates evolution.

Evolution expands all.

Wanting to make a lot of money doesn't make you greedy or a bad person.

In my experience good people do really good things with money.

This is often a construct that simply keeps good people coasting by financially instead of truly being able to make a larger impact.

And it creates a feeling of living a half life.

Not quite living up to our fullest potential.

Which our desires guide us to.

So when we are willing to own desire as good, we're willing to know what we want and we're willing to move in alignment with them, we begin creating and living a life in alignment with our continually expanding potential.

When we can release shame and learn to embrace and even lust for a good life, without lack, this is the sweet spot.

This is where we hold a firm and solid energy of desire.

This is where we experience swift and potent manifestation.

What does desire actually feel like?

Knowing this is important to distinguish desire from lack.

When we're in lack we perpetuate lack in our experiences.

Not just on the level of energetic attraction but also our brains continue to pull on and reinforce the concept of never having enough or not yet having something and it feeling bad.

Which keeps us stuck in a cycle of recreating lack, again and again and again.

And perpetually experiencing never getting what we want next.

In order for this to shift, we need a pattern interrupt.

We have to do something new and different.

And this is play and staying in desire.

Often times people will feel like they want something and they will feel tension, pressure, anxiety, and a feeling of need.

This feeling of need is a clear indicator of lack.

I've seen this with myself and clients over the years.

Do you actually *need* to make $100,000.00/ month or do you just want it?

I'll give you a hint.

It's always that they just want it.

But because they have a moment of not yet having it, and recognizing that they don't have it, they can sometimes slip into an energy that's overly aware of it's absence and start to feel like they're "lacking" something.

Desire is the sensation that when you're in it, you feel like you already have it.

There is no "need" there is no "lack"

But many will continually take their desires and make them into needs.

When we can stop doing this, we can sustain desire and this frequency is where things move REALLY fast.

In desire you experience a feeling as though you already have it, even though you technically don't yet in the physical.

This is that clean desire frequency we're going for.

I'll give you a simple example: Let's pretend you're craving some French fries.

I personally love anything potato or sweet potato so this is a good one for me.

My fiancé will often say that I'm going to turn into one.

I don't disagree.

But I digress.

So you're thinking about French fries, but you don't yet have them.

Your mouth begins salivating, as if it's already about to devour them.

You think about what it's like to eat some French fries.

You enjoy the idea of them.

Yet, there are no French fries in front of you.

Now replace that with money, or whatever else you want.

Compared to need.

Let's use the same French fry approach because this will clearly will get us places.

You're craving French fries, and don't yet have them.

Your mind begins to wonder where you could get some.

You start to feel agitated that you don't have them.

Maybe even annoyed by the fact that you wanted them, and don't have them.

This is lack.

We can steer into desire or lack at the idea of anything we want, like wealth.

The idea of wealthy and becoming a wealthy woman can turn you on and light you up or shut you down, piss you off, and make you feel defeated.

Whether you're operating in actual desire or lack will be the determining factor.

Learning to distinguish between these 2 feelings and then intentionally steering towards desire is where you create and maintain magnetism towards your desires.

From the energy of lack, most people try and overcompensate with force.

Which is incredibly draining and exhausting because we're trying to overcome and push against not having something we want and it just doesn't yield the same level of results and ease that's available to us when we're in magnetic desire.

This is where you feel like you're giving something 110% of your energy for a 10% return.

Because we can't overcompensate for lack of alignment.

Or this is where people pull the energetic plug.

Meaning, they stop letting themselves want what they want out of fear of being disappointed because they're stuck in the feeling of lacking what they want.

Usually this creates an internal narrative of "fuck it, why try? I'm just going to be disappointed anyways."

Or "It never works for me, so what's the point?"

This is when the ego has taken over to keep you safe.

It's keeping you safe from feeling feelings of potential disappointment or maybe even rejection.

When we can see this for what it is, and keep holding the energy of desire, we become truly powerful.

That saying of "Everything you want is on the other side of your comfort zone."

It's true.

But it's more like your ego's comfort zone.

Because your heart and soul is deeply comfortable in what you desire.

So many people live their lives protecting themselves from failure by not allowing themselves to hold and sustain the sensation of desire simply because they're afraid of it not working.

True power is when we can handle temporary disappointment or not having it "yet," or being rejected, and still keep holding it and moving in alignment with it.

This whole life thing is a work in progress for all of us.

The more we can understand that and keep showing up WHILE holding the frequency of desire, the more you are going to blow your mind.

The more life is going to open to you.

Something I like to say as an example of this is:

When you know you can handle any potential wave, you allow yourself to play deeper and deeper in the ocean of abundance.

The waves happen for all of us.

Some of us get out of the water, where some of us lean in and go deeper in.

The difference between the two is in the choice to keep moving and the choice to keep holding it.

The choice to keep wanting it and moving in alignment with it, instead of dropping the energetic ball of desire.

So to recap, you have to let yourself want because wanting is good.

Desire is where we expand for ourselves, those around us, and the collective.

Desire is not lack, these are two separate frequencies.

You can continue to hold the sensation of desire in your being, regardless of waves.

And life and money will open to you in ways you've never experienced before.

Here's some exercises I've given clients on desire to help you anchor this in.

Do you feel good and safe in desire?

_____

_____

_____

_____

_____

_____

If yes, how does it feel? If no, why don't I?

_____

_____

_____

_____

_____

_____

When and why do I make my desires a need?

_____

_____

_____

_____

_____

_____

Often we will make our desires a need because we're programmed to think we can't just have what we want, simply for wanting it.

So we must justify why we "need" it.

But when we're willing to release need and play fully in desire, life and money will crack open for you.

6

CREATING EMBODIED WEALTH

The energy of money is something I'm asked about a lot in some context or another.

And what is helpful to understand is that money is a dance.

It's something we must learn to move with and be in relationship with in order to continually grow in this area.

In my experience of creating wealth the work has always started from the inside out.

This is why I teach embodied wealth.

It's not solely internal or external, it's both. But it starts from within.

I cultivate my inner world so deliciously and powerfully and allow it to ooze out naturally.

From here, my energy is potent and my actions are swift and meaningful.

From here, we FEEL pulled instead of feeling like we're pushing or overcoming something in our physical world.

Because our desires are a cooperative force, meaning, when we want it, it wants us.

And when we can powerfully cultivate our inner world and drip in the desire and frequencies of what we want, they will pull on us cleanly and powerfully.

This is where the ideas with all the "YUM I want to do that RIGHT NOW!" feelings come from. It doesn't mean it can't feel scary or edgy but it will feel sexy and fuck yes.

When we bury our desire for more, our desire will still pull on us, they just might pull us into all the bullshit that's in the way of getting there, also known as the patterns we've buried our desires under.

It's a good thing, we either get to navigate it and emerge on the other side or transmute them with power and grace while we continue to glide forward.

Sometimes ease calls you through something feeling hard.

From here we get to open to more because we must open to it- instead of try and fight and push through.

Sometimes abundance pulls you through lack.

From here we get to open to more because we must- instead of try and fight and push through.

It's all an opportunity to open to more and step deeper and deeper into a beautiful and abundant life.

Opening and surrendering is not quitting or giving up, it's a shift in your energy to opening and trusting.

I live by life by money is responding to us. Because it is ;)

The energy of money is not inherently one thing or another.

It will take different roles.

But it is always responding to us.

I have feelings and established belief systems (through practice) around money taking this role of wanting to show up for me and deeply support and even spoil me. Because I've allowed life to open me to these beliefs.

And my job is to simply be available to receive it.

And other times, money is waiting on me to move.

AKA when you get caught up in some fuck shit and stop the flow because you get in your head, second guess yourself, or whatever else.

This can create a feeling of feeling like you're waiting.

And this is stagnant AF (as fuck) ;)

What a lot of people do is "wait on money"

When it's time to dance.

You'll notice this is occurring when you start to experience financial stagnation.

Yes, regardless of your career path.

Money isn't limited to the job you work or the career you have, it has an infinite amount of ways it can flow in.

I've seen time and time again, those who are available to this dance will often get unexpected raises or better job opportunities.

I've had clients win 6 figures on scratch off tickets.

And business owners go to the next level.

In my experience of growing a 7 figure business, I had to throw the habit of waiting on money, in the trash.

In recognizing that I wanted to create an intentional and beautiful life I had to do just that, create it.

I had to allow the power of my desire to pull me and step out in front of the current dynamics that were in play and do something differently.

This is how we create space to receive even more.

The first time I really started playing with this concept was when I began investing in my business and hiring mentors.

I couldn't wait until it felt like the easiest and most convenient thing.

My job is not to to control when it's aligned or to control the circumstances of alignment, but to be aligned.

And to move when I know it's aligned.

Sometimes that aligned movement feels sexy, effortless, and like a deep "fuck yes!"

Sometimes it feels a little edgy, crunchy, scary or bat shit crazy.

But that deeper inner knowing of "this is the move" is the alignment.

What I've seen in myself and my clients over the years is this becomes the dance of money.

Sometimes we must lean in and sometimes we must lean back to continue the flow of money.

This is the dance.

And knowing when it is aligned to lean in or lean back is the art of the on going process.

Much like real dancing we have to stay in tune with the movement and intuition of the moment.

Surrender to it fully and be there in that moment to feel the alignment.

We don't do for the sake of doing, we tune in and move intentionally and in alignment.

Equally we don't unplug and hide and pretend it's the aligned lean back and opening.

We honor the pulse of the moment.

The presence of the dance.

When I first invested in my business, I was freshly living on my own.

I had maybe $200 to my name with a credit card that had a $200 limit.

I was freshly new to the whole adult thing.

Rent was due soon, I had to buy groceries soon, it wasn't a logical time to invest money into anything.

Yet, the pull was there.

Often people will say "it's not the right time."

And I say, that's not for you to decide, when life calls you, when your inner fuck yes speaks, you listen and move. It's not about a right or wrong time. It's about following the inner fuck yes.

I invested $200 which at the time felt like A LOT.

And legally committed to the program that was $200/month for 12 months.

I laughed at how irresponsible and crazy I felt for doing it.

But the thing is, it was only irresponsible if I planned on it not working.

If I planned on staying at the same level.

Which I sure as shit wasn't planning on doing.

My brain said "What if we can't pay our bills?"

And I laughed and said "Well I guess I better make some money then!"

It was "irresponsible"

Yet, it just felt right.

And I trusted that.

I didn't give my brain an out so it had no choice but to get on board with the up level and work in alignment with me instead of working on "keeping me safe."

When we don't give our mind the option for it to not work, it will use all of it resourcefulness towards it working instead of preparing plan B.

Over the next few weeks, I made more money than I ever had before.

I made a few thousand dollars which was the most I had made before, at that point in time.

This was an example of me going out in front of the current dynamic to create a new one.

I didn't tell anyone because I knew the well meaning people in my life would either be scared for me, or try and talk me out of it.

And my level of confidence in what I was doing wasn't strong enough to hold it in the presence of people who may have doubted it or me.

Now, I substantially out earn those well meaning people.

This isn't to flex or brag, this is a reminder to trust yourself.

You have guidance inside of you that other people can't feel because they aren't you.

Which means they don't want what you want, the way you want it, and they can't feel the guidance of your inner fuck yes.

They can't validate it for you.

Only you really know, because you can feel it.

The only people I listen to are those who make way more than I do, and are doing it in a way that aligns with my heart and values and even then it runs through my inner guidance system.

I'm not interested in a lot of money with a lot of overworking and hustling and no time for living.

I'm not interested with things that feel icky in my system.

I want the alignment, heart, and spaciousness.

And this is exactly what I have created and continue to build upon.

Equally we must be in tune with the aligned lean back.

The aligned lean back is when we've done our part and now we must lead back and be available to receive.

We can also say, this is when we trust.

Sometimes people ask me "How do I trust?"

And I say, "How do you stop drinking water?"

You just do.

When you stop overthinking it, you realize that you do in fact know how.

The aligned lean back is tuning into the inner stillness and guidance instead of the part of you that feels like it needs it NOW and you need to franticly push and do all the things or else.

This chokeholds our ability to receive.

I've often shared with my clients this analogy.

You've invited a lot of friends over to a party.

The invites are out, your job is to prepare the party and have a good time as people begin to roll in.

This is an especially relevant analogy because as I write this chapter, I'm less than 2 months out from getting married and the RSVPs are rolling in. YIPPIE

When we choke hold, we are metaphorically standing in the doorway yelling "HELLLOOOOO!?!?!?!? IS ANYONE COMING OR WHAT!?" And there in, don't allow space in the door way.

So no matter how many people are waiting to cross the threshold and come to your party, they literally can't fit through the doorway because you're occupying all of the space.

We have to leave room for people to come inside.

We have to have energetic room for money.

We have to plant the seeds and let them grow

And keep partying while people begin showing up.

So live your damn life.

Take a bath.

And stop feeling so shitty about it.

Okay? Love you.

7

SELF SOURCING POWER

Power is something I talk a lot about and teach on in my work.

It's something important to understand in order to continually improve our financial circumstances.

And feel sexy doing it.

In order to utilize and understand energetic and personal power we first have to know what it means.

Your power is the ability to sustain and hold the embodied frequencies of what you want unconditionally.

It's your ability to self source.

Which means, independent of your circumstances.

This isn't easy at first when you're used to reacting to the totality of your life.

It's called power because it takes energetic power, sourced from self, not from our circumstances or conditions, in order to hold it and hold it continually.

It's easy for most people to hold their power and sustain certainty and confidence when things are exactly as they want and feel they should be, but cultivating power before, that is true power, this is self sourcing.

This doesn't mean we won't have times where we drop it, or we wobble.

It means we continually refine and self source so we can handle and hold more and more of all that we desire.

Which means we can't make what we desire the source of how we want to feel.

That's our job.

We are powerful enough to do that.

The things we want get to add to it and be a match to us but they can't be the source or you will be in for an unnecessarily bumpy ride.

Our power is the energetic landing strip for the planes of our desires, that they need in order to land.

I'm not a pilot but I have flown on my fair share of airplanes over the years.

And I don't see pilots landing without knowing there's a landing strip available for them to safely land the plane and passengers inside.

Our desires are the same.

They want a solid place to land.

This means we have to energetically prepare to hold them.

This is when we experience the ease factor.

The ability to hold what we want with ease.

Because we are energetically more powerful.

And therefore it doesn't feel hard to us.

Much like when we first pick up a heavier weight, our bodies eventually adapt if we keep picking it up, and we can eventually hold it with ease.

We've prepared the landing strip and now the plane of our desires can glide in and land smoothly.

I didn't just have to learn how to hold this, in sustaining feelings of safety around money in the beginning of my journey, but I have had to continually deepen this work in order to call in and sustain higher and higher levels of receiving and having.

At a point I was desiring overflow with money.

Overflow, meaning, I paid for all that I needed, all that I wanted, and I still had a lot of money in the bank.

I was already living in overflow but not to the extent the I wanted to....yet.

For me, at the time, having 6 figures in the bank after doing all that I needed and all that I wanted, THAT would be real overflow.

But I didn't have it yet.

I felt into what does overflow ACTUALLY feel like.

I felt into paying all of my bills and business expenses and all the things.

I felt into paying for all that I wanted.

Investing the money I wanted to invest.

Donating the money I wanted to donate.

And still having over $100,000.00 in the bank.

It felt more open, it felt more spacious.

And I realized I wasn't feeling that feeling on going, in my day to day life.

This was the gap in my energetic power.

My energetic landing strip wasn't big enough for more because I wasn't holding that energy within myself, independent of circumstances, sourced completely from myself.

I was in a pattern of *waiting* to have more before I felt that way.

I realized that when I was paying off my credit cards that my default setting was a feeling of "My bank account is going to go down. That's fine. I still have a good amount. I'll be okay."

And that was totally okay, but that, THAT, was NOT overflow.

That was the energy of I'll be fine.

And that didn't feel sexy.

Nor was it aligned with having more.

So I began playing with holding the energy that I felt before, when I played with having a lot more left over.

I practiced, in moments through out my day, feeling and holding the feelings of spaciousness, a lot left over, turned on by having 6 figures in the bank after all of that.

I practiced holding that feeling when I spent money, when I invested money, when I transferred money from one account to another.

And I began holding it more and more.

And naturally more and more started coming in.

I want to be clear here.

I didn't withhold my spending or investing or playing with money.

I didn't manipulate the circumstances at all.

I did what I wanted and held this energy.

It didn't matter how much I was spending or investing, more just kept coming in.

I watched my account grow and grow until it hit 6 figures.

I kept holding the energy instead of getting attached and needy and protective of it.

I could have fallen into an energy where I stopped flowing my dollars out of fear of it dipping back below 6 figures.

But I chose not to.

I chose to hold the energy and kept flowing my dollars.

And some how, some way, I just didn't dip below it.

It just kept coming in and adding up to where I wanted it to be.

Now my standard for what I keep in the bank is a lot higher than this.

But It's because I've intentionally expanded on this energy.

I naturally allowed desire to come forward for more.

And would play with the way it felt and work on embodying it before it was here.

And holding it.

And when I would drop it, I would simply plug back in.

I want to highlight something important here,

I had to choose to be in this energy.

Literally just decide and not make it any more complicated than that.

I had to choose to be in this energy simply because I wanted to and that was the only reason I needed.

When you get to a point of sustaining your needs being met by money, you have to transition out of need being a reason why you choose to hold the energy.

You choose to because you choose to.

You want to and that's the only reason you need to.

When we stay connected to the visceral feelings of what we want we don't need to justify why we can receive it.

We just can because we want to.

I noticed that in order to step deeper into having more and more money I had to harness this energy of choosing it.

That any part of me that felt I could only hold it if it was "justified" by need, was simply me not realizing I was worthy of having more simply because I wanted to.

I didn't do some deep ritual around clearing this, I just chose to hold it because it was a desire and NOT a need and this was all I needed to do in order for this energy to clear out of me.

I deepened this energy into receiving 6 figures a month.

My first 6 figure month in business was just over $144,000.00 cash received in one month.

It didn't make "sense" I didn't try to manipulate anything to receive it.

It came in because I allowed myself to fully listen to the pulse of my desires in every moment.

I wanted new clothes, so I bought some.

I wanted to take a trip and fly first class and have the time of my life with my fiancé, so I booked it and did it.

I took a week off and listened to the impulses of my desires and completely trusted them.

I gave my team members in my business a raise.

I gave money to strangers, donated and shared from alignment.

And it added up to more and more.

Here's the next piece..

I did it and made it all mean that it was adding up to what I wanted.

I didn't do it so that it would add up to more.

I did it because I wanted to and then I decided it would add up to more.

This is an important distinction.

You can't trick the universe.

You don't do it because you think it'll trick the universe into giving you more money.

"SEE! LOOK AT ME UNIVERSE I'M BEING NICE AND BRAVE WILL YOU PLEASE REWARD ME WITH SOME MORE MONEY NOW?!? K THANKS!!!" <<< Not how it works, though I know many have tried.

You do it because it's a genuine desire of your heart in the moment.

Another sneaky way we try and trick the universe is we try and take life long desires and make them all happen RIGHT NOW.

This is lack.

This is us not fully trusting the moment.

This is us not trusting the future.

It's lack because it's trying to get it all now instead of trusting the continual flow of forever.

When we trust the continual flow of forever we don't typically try and buy the yacht on day 1.

Meaning, we don't need to have it now in order to know we're going to have it.

We trust and tune into the desire of the moment and trust it and walk in alignment with it.

Attaching to loss in our spending (another way we drop our power)

Something people can do, I know because I used to do this ;)

Is they can attach to a feeling of loss with their actions.

In how they flow their dollars, in how they spend their time, or in how they live their life and make it mean they can't have more and make it mean that it's adding up to having less.

This is attaching to the idea of losing something.

I decided to stop doing that.

And what happened in just 1 month of time was a little over $60,000.00 cash in one month to the next month being $144,000.00 cash

Cash meaning, not sales, actual income that came in, in that month, before taxes.

Here's how we attach to loss.

We spend the money and we have a feeling response.

However subtle, or not so subtle, feelings of "this means I will have less."

For those who are programming themselves out of scarcity, this can bring up deeper feelings of fear of losing it all.

This often leads to trying to control the money, spend less, hold onto it more, etc.

Which is lack and severely closing off your receiving, just fyi.

They make it mean that the ways they spend money (or hold money) or the way they work or don't work is adding down instead of adding up.

Adding down to less and less until they're in a situation of struggle.

But we have the option of changing what we make things mean.

The voice of desire is an energy that once we trust and live from will always add up to more and more and more.

It will blow your mind at how you do what you want and earn what you want in alignment with each other.

This brings us into spending.

I have done what is considered "irresponsible" in regards to money and it's always added up to more and more.

I understand that what is actually responsible is me listening to my soul over rules from other people.

Because I understand the energy underneath it all. It's not about how we spend or how much we spend *GASP*

Don't throw the book at the wall, please.

It's about how we feel when we spend.

It's about what we believe about our spending.

It's about what we make it mean.

Back when I was making around $20k a month in my business I invested $20k in one month and paid it off in one month because I held a firm energy of being met by money.

It was an edge for me but it felt right and aligned so I trusted it and just held the energy because I decided to.

That month I made over $40k. (For the first time)

We can actually retrain ourselves to feel deeply abundant anytime we spend and invest our money.

For me, I look at every time I spend my money as an investment.

And I've decided a long time ago, that all of my investments yield a large return.

When I buy myself clothes, it's an investment in me feeling sexy and yummy and playing in the physical world from this energy.

When I buy myself a car, it's an investment in my joy.

I love vroom vrooming in my sexy car with the sunroof open.

Let me make this clear, it's an investment into it, not the source of it.

Stuff isn't a source of happiness. But that doesn't mean you can't enjoy it.

Let's drop any shame or guilt around that, right now.

You're meant to live a good life and if you want nice shit around you, you're allowed.

Just don't make it the source. This is when people become deeply unhappy and unfulfilled.

God wants us to have fun with the human experience.

When I spend money on experiences, travel, etc.

It's an investment.

When I hire mentors, it's an investment in my growth.

These all yield a return.

When I allow myself to hold the energy of what I stand for.

Which is a big and beautiful life and flow my dollars accordingly.

I yield a return.

So from here, as money flows continually in and out, it's always adding up to more and more and more and more.

So I invite you into the perspective of, what if you played with every purchase as an investment into something, that yielded a return, not only energetically but this added up to a financial return.

Because as you live your life energetically investing in and living in alignment with your abundance.

You yield more abundance.

Now I would like you to think about the last time you spent money...

How did you feel?

If you could put words to it, what is it saying?

_____

_____

_____

If it wasn't a sexy feeling, let me ask you this.

If you were in your currently desired financial circumstances how would you have felt in spending?

_____

_____

_____

_____

This is the gap in your power and therefore mirrored in your circumstances.

But the cool part about life is, it's always giving you reasons to want more.

Closing the gap is how we receive more,

This is what you must play with and play with embodying as you spend, invest, receive, all of it.

Apply it to any future handlings of money.

Whether it's paying your bills, looking at your bank accounts, investing money in your business, life, or future.

You've got this.

The same goes for debt, firstly debt isn't a bad thing. Our society makes debt the literal devil and this is unnecessary and not helpful.

Debt, like money, can be a very amazing tool.

I have personally utilized debt and paying it off easily was about feeling really clean and solid in how I utilized it. If I had any resistance, resentment, or guilt, it would linger.

I've seen this over the years with clients, no matter how much they would make or how much money they would pay towards debt, they would end up back in the same amount of debt. It wasn't until they felt really clean and grateful about how they were spending their money and utilizing credit that they could stay out of debt.

So I invite you to sit down and BE with all of your purchases and investments and feel really fucking good about all of them.

You can't go back in time and undue it, but you can get your energy behind it now, feel really grateful for it, be happy about the decision you made (because YES you can trust yourself) and don't need to create any weird patterns of blocking money because you think you can't trust yourself. So let's just avoid that, please and thank you.

Release any guilt, feel elated and turned on by every past and future purchase.

Watch money chase you like the sexy thing you are, from this energy.

8

EASE WITH MONEY

When we get attached to the idea that it has to be hard we forget that we are worthy of ease accompanying our experience of money.

I've noticed on the subject of money that for many, it's wired into us from the belief systems of our society, family, jobs, and environments, that making a lot of money is really hard.

When I was younger I wondered if this HAD to be true and began exploring other options.

With money being something we have a relationship to and relationships are moldable and can shift dynamics, it just made sense to explore other options.

Because frankly I didn't desire hard for the sake of hard.

The idea of that made me want to throw up and take a nap from exhaustion just thinking about it.

Just because people decided it had to be an experience that accompanied money didn't seem like a good enough reason to me.

I became curious if money could actually be easy.

This curiosity led to a willingness to actually explore and be open to money as an extension of ease.

Because if my desires are God given because they're meant for me, it didn't make sense to take ease off the table.

This led me to a whole different dynamic within my relationship to, and experience of money.

I started wondering how people who grew up differently than I did, thought about and experienced money, they seemed to have a lot less drama with it.

People who never worried about money, people who always had their wants and needs met without question.

An upbringing where a good relationship with money was normal.

And I started bringing in these ideas to shift my experience of money.

When I saw people who had a lot of money I would pay attention to how they were with it.

I would pull from what felt good knowing that because it felt good to me, that these were breadcrumbs leading me to my aligned relationship with money.

I would notice they didn't have the same drama I had learned to associate with the experience of money.

So I adopted their way of thinking.

I also saw how some people had different kinds of drama with money, I left those because, no thank you.

I would pay attention to how they would think and see often that it was different than the way I thought

Because I was previously programmed to think differently about money based on past experiences and my upbringing of it.

I began seeing where I wasn't allowing myself to think and behave in alignment with the experience of money I wanted because I didn't feel worthy of it.

It was not a conscious feeling or a thought playing on loop in my head that said "I'm not worthy." or "I don't feel worthy."

It was a feeling and it was in how I behaved.

I didn't even consciously know this was how I felt until I felt into it deeper and explored it and questioned what I was feeling habitually and why.

It showed up as discomfort and contraction around receiving and a disconnect to expecting to be deeply supported by money.

And naturally when we contract, which means we're energetically closing, we're blocking our ability to receive more.

I didn't feel worthy of it because it wasn't normalized for me or normal to me.

If having lots of money with ease was "special" (because it was to me)

And I was normal, to myself

It computed that I wasn't worthy of it

The mind can draw some weird and occasionally fucked up and inaccurate conclusions and we can unconsciously live in alignment with them and create more circumstances to reenforce these limiting ideas.

This unworthy feeling kept me off of the frequency of having a better experience of money

Having more and having more with ease

Feeling unworthy will keep up from experiencing deeper ease and many will block becoming wealthy and block ease because they will feel uncomfortable being witnessed in wealth or ease.

The idea of being witnessed in ease of wealth creation can bring a fear of people questioning if you deserve it, and if some part of you is already believing that, you'll block wealth from ease.

From here, you'll either not let yourself receive, only receive very little, or you'll let yourself receive after you feel you can justify it to yourself and or others.

Something I say to my clients is, "It's easy to own it when no one is questioning or second guessing you, but how would you feel if they did?"

Would you still feel the innate worthiness of you and your ability to have and receive a shit ton of money and build real wealth for yourself?

If not, we need to look at why and clean that shit up. ;)

When you're able to stand in who you, what you have, and own what you get to have and create in the midst of people who "don't get it," in the midst of people who project their fears, doubts, and insecurities, onto you, you are truly powerful.

It doesn't mean you have to hang out with these kinds of people, because obviously we all want cool and nice friends. But you know that you can handle it and hold your worth.

Like I mentioned earlier, whether it's a family member, friend, or stranger on the internet.

Someone who can own this energy gives a lot of people a lot of permission to own their worth and desire for more.

What I eventually came to realize was that it was never that I wasn't worthy, it was that it just wasn't normalized for me.

And I could make having a lot of money become normal for me.

I've seen this pattern in many people over the years

When we don't feel worthy we will often feel the need to "prove" that we are

To "earn" abundance

To justify why we have it or should have it

Instead of feel inherently worthy of abundance

And money will respond to us on these frequencies.

When becoming someone who desires to have ease with money, we will begin to notice and unravel the ways in which we make it unnecessarily hard.

With this, the frequencies of ease is something we invite in and have a continual relationship with.

In stepping deeper and deeper into ease we will sometimes need to unconsciously make it hard to see how we're not allowing ourselves to go deeper into ease.

Our unconscious will make itself known by curating circumstances and conditions to become conscious.

The contrast of something feeling hard provides the experience to deepen into more ease on the other side.

But ease is still the home you get to return to and deepen in continually, and infinitely.

When we're aware of this we can see where we're attaching to hard and release it to allow in ease.

What I often end up seeing is many who set up camp in what feels hard instead of seeing it as a gateway into deeper ease.

Because it is seen as noble and honorable in many settings to do hard things.

Sure it's amazing to see people overcome but I don't believe in bringing hard in for the sake of it being hard for some fucked up reason.

This is when we lean into unnecessary suffering that is heavily normalized in our society.

Which for many of the people who come into my world, we don't resonate with.

We want to make money in alignment with our heart, purpose, pleasure, ease, and flow.

From here, we can have a really clean energy with being of service, because our desire to serve is uninterrupted.

We don't resonate with wealth at the expense of anything important to us and still believe in wealth.

Because we're meant to welcome in and be a part of a new paradigm with money.

Not need to step outside of what we desire in order to receive and then squeak in pleasure.

I've found that actually when we allow ourselves to receive in alignment with how we want to receive, we pull in substantially more abundance because we have more energetic capacity to receive and hold it.

Where as when we're pulling money into our realities out of alignment with ourselves, we don't have enough energy to take care of ourselves deeply, create beautiful relationships and lives and still hold space for massive abundance.

Because what we believe about how to make money requires us to step outside of alignment with ourselves.

But when we invite in ease with money, money amplifies what's important to us, and comes in as an extension of us prioritizing what matters.

Now I want you to get clear on some important things,

How do you want receiving money to feel to you?

_____

_____

_____

_____

_____

What limiting ideas do you have about how money has to be earned by you and in your life?

_____

_____

_____

_____

Is there anything you believe is required of you that you that doesn't feel sexy?

If so, what is it?

_____

_____

_____

_____

Why do you believe this?

_____

_____

_____

_____

Where did this belief come from?

_____

_____

_____

_____

Knowing that your relationship with money is sacred and unique to you, what do you choose to change and practice, about what you believe about how money can work for you?

_____

_____

_____

_____

What do you need to release and what gets to take it's place?

_____

_____

_____

What if you could just receive because you wanted to and there was nothing to prove?

_____

_____

_____

_____

What does money get to be an extension of for you in your life?

_____

_____

_____

_____

The energy of ease, is not about not doing anything. It's about knowing you're worthy of ease. Do not confuse ease for stagnation and avoidance. From ease, you will move but it will feel sexy, powerful and flowy, not doing for the sake of feeling like you need to in order to prove you deserve more or because you must do x to receive y.

You get to have it because you do, then you get to do what you want. From here, you're freed up a lot of your creative energy and will want to…. CREATE.

You're doing things that you WANT to be doing, that feels fuck yes, that give you life, turn you on and light you up, and dollars flow in.

You get to receive because you want to and you get to do things and build your life and vision because it's yummy and fun.

8

WHEN IS IT GOING
TO HAPPEN?

There was a time when I realized that it wasn't so much about time and it was more about maintaining being an energetic match and just staying open to the magic of life and money flowing in and blowing my mind, regardless of time.

I would often check in, what day is it? How many days are left this week? This month? This year? Do I have time? Do I have enough time to receive/create what I want?

And from here I would not only experience a shortage of time and feeling like a serious psycho busy person. I also experienced my openness to life and money blowing my mind seriously dwindling based on time.

And money would flow in alignment with my expectations of what seemed reasonable based on "how much time was left."

I wasn't open to what was illogical, and me and the people I attract in my world want MAGIC. Everything being completely linear feels boring and makes us the complete opposite of wet and turned on for life.

We want to have a solid relationship with continually raising the bar on what's logical for us and always being open to what's possible and what's mind blowing.

When we aren't open to what's possible we don't receive it.

From this place we can only receive based on what's logical for us.

SNOOZE! Too much of this makes no room for playing with possibilities and makes for a dull girl

I began to realize a few very important things

How often I would drop my energy based on time because it just felt logical!

So I literally just decided to stop doing this.

The income growth I've experienced this year occurred on the other side of this.

I decided I would not drop my energy because of time and it didn't matter how the month, the launch, the quarter, the year, etc. ended.

I was going to hold the energy and stay open anyways and either way.

At first I just felt more powerful, and I was still receiving in alignment with what felt logical, which was pretty damn good, either way I wasn't checking in based on time.

Then, for a few months in a row my income began increasing, month over month.

Which in the past I was attached to and wouldn't always experience.

Then, $60k to $144k in one month. A quantum leap.

Because I wasn't using time as a limitation and money responded, showed up in the same frequency.

A quantum leap.... Something Joe Dispenza talks about in his teachings, the quantum field doesn't operate on time, it operates on frequencies. There is no separation.

Time occurs when we move through space. But in the quantum field there is just the void of nothing and everything. Infinite possibilities.

When we drop the attachment to time, we can open to limitless possibilities, also known as, being open to what's possible.

But if we're constantly using time as a limitation, we can't be open to it.

The vibe is, open to the infinite magic, I'm open to life and money blowing my mind. I get to hold and continue to play in what I desire, with non-attachment to when. I will shift what needs to be shifted as it arises and plug back into desire.

From my attachment to time, I realized I popped in and out of desire because I was worried about my ability to be able to receive/create what I wanted by a certain point in time. And that just felt silly. Why would I unplug from my desire simply because I was worried that I wouldn't be able to do it by x point in time?

Because some deeper part of me was worried that if I gave it my all and held it, I would be massively disappointed.

And have nothing to blame.

But it we stopped doing this, we would just hold the energy indefinitely.

And from here, receive a lot more, a lot faster.

If we don't believe we can have something within a certain period of time, we tend to drop the energy.

This flip flopping of being in and out of alignment with our desires tends to make it take longer.

But when we think we can have it at some point, without the pressure of an arbitrary timeline, we tend to keep holding the energy of what we want, without lack and without unplugging.

This is where I welcome in "the moment before."

This is a concept I teach on in relationship to time with money.

Is it actually "not working" or are you just in the moment before it happens.

This realization changed everything for me.

Just like those few months where it was still happening in alignment with my logic, pretty damn good, but not blowing my mind with infinite possibilities.

The thing is, if and when your logical baseline is still pretty damn good compared to the average person, you still get to dance on your leading edge of expansion in your life and want more.

Mediocrity isn't your style.

And we all have a personal current standard of mediocrity.

Your job is to have high standards and not settle.

With my logical baseline not yet blowing my mind, I could have dropped it because of "how long it was taking."

I realized just how often my own mind attached to the idea of something not working simply because it hadn't happened yet.

And if I'm in the energy of it not working, it can't work.

I realized how often this thought process sabotaged literally everything.

It threw my energy into a place of "it's not working."

And from here, my defense mechanisms would kick in.

I would feel defeated and start slowing down my momentum.

I would second guess myself and start moving a lot slower, or try and figure out what the problem was, and a lot of the time there wasn't one.

And I would just overall be energetically unavailable to receive what I wanted.

I would check in- again and again and stop the momentum.

When instead all I had to do was keep moving towards what I wanted to the best of my ability and trust it all to add up and unfold when it did.

The moment before concept is the idea of taking what we learn in hindsight and bringing it into foresight in the moment.

Where we integrate the knowing of something coming, before it comes.

So many times people spend their time worrying about whether or not something is going to happen, they spend so much mental energy on "if" and "when," that they unplug from desire and plug into fear and doubt.

The thing is we can only ever highly anticipate the timing of what we want, but we only know for sure until we're already on the other side of the moment of receiving it.

We can have everything lined up perfectly, but we still don't ever actually know when the moment of receiving is, until it's already passed and we're looking back on it.

We can look back on the previous moment and realize, "oh hey that was when it happened."

But by that point in time, it's already passed and we're on the other side.

And the receiving is now a memory of the recent past.

This realization changed things for me because I thought back on the moments before something epic happened and I started asking myself how I was thinking and feeling and what I was anticipating in that moment.

How this thing was going to happen either way, because it did.

And I had a choice of how I could respond to the moment before.

I could be in lack, worry, self doubt, etc. and from here, obviously delay it.

Or I could focus on something else.

Which was- How do I want to remember the moment before?

How do I want to feel crossing into these inevitable milestones?

Sure I'm not just sitting on my pretty little ass waiting around.

This isn't a point on "waiting" for anything.

If we're feeling like we're waiting on something, we're not in alignment.

We're in lack and we're not leading life, we're waiting on life.

I can sit on my pretty little ass and not feel like I'm waiting.

Equally, I can be doing all the things and feel like I'm waiting on something.

I'm doing the best I can with what I desire in the moment and walking in alignment with it.

And I know that as long as I keep going, I will continue to create all that I desire.

Or I'm in an aligned lean back.

But either way, my energy is in motion.

The vibe is, what keeps my energy in motion.

The yummy feeling on acting on inspired actions.

The yummy feeling of playing in my life.

The yummy feeling of the aligned lean back.

So, how do I want to feel in the moment before?

Is there actually an issue?

Is there actually something that needs to be adjusted?

Or am I just in the moment before?

So many people waste this moment before by doubting and worrying and therein move themselves out of alignment with the moment of receiving more and more.

But when we change our relationship to the moment before, we tend to have a lot more moments of receiving.

The paradox is when we release our attachment to "when" it comes in faster.

Because we're no longer operating based on a limiting idea of a linear timeline.

When we tend to operate in an overly linear way, we tend to expect in a very linear and logical way as well.

Which keeps us in the field of receiving in alignment with what we believe makes sense.

With what we believe is "logical" for us to receive.

And typically what feels logical for us, often times, will be in alignment with the past.

What we have received already, before.

On the timelines we've received them.

Which doesn't open us to what's available that is beyond our scope of logic.

And you, my love, are here for a big and beautiful life beyond what you could ever imagine.

With life, with money, with all of it.

You are worthy.

You are powerful.

You get to be wealthy.

You get to take this life thing as far as you want.

I'm cheering you on.

I believe in you.

I love you.

And you're sexy.

RESOURCES

Free resources inside Genevieve's free facebook community-The Rich Spiritual Money Bitches, inside there is an endless supply of free masterclasses and content, which are frequently added to.

OTHER RESOURCES

1:1 private mentorship- for spiritual entrepreneurs and business owners wanting to play in my energy at the highest level of support

Get lit with money bitch- 8 module course on healing your relationship with money

Potency- 3 module program on how to make money from the quantum field for quantum leaping your income

Magnetic- 4 module program on how to continually attract and book high end paying soul aligned fuck yes clients.

LOW COST TRAININGS

Money manifestation 101

From Debt to overflow like a sexy bitch

Collapsing time with money

The Upward Spiral- becoming the unstoppable woman who's always expanding her wealth

SOCIAL MEDIA

Instagram: https://www.instagram.com/genevieverackham/

Facebook page- https://www.facebook.com/genevieve.lightworker/

Facebook group- https://www.facebook.com/groups/richspiritualmoney

ACKNOWLEDGMENTS

Kevin- Thank you for always being my biggest supporter, believing in me, loving me, holding me, through it all. Your heart inspires me every day. You're hilarious and SO freaking smart and I'm so grateful to have a beautiful man with such a beautiful mind and heart in my life and I can't wait to marry you! You are the love of my life.

Dad- Thank you for growing with me. Thank you for thinking bigger just because you love and believe in me. I love having you in my life as I grow. And thank you for never letting me win at chess growing up, even though it deeply pissed me off. XD

Mom- Thank you for expanding me. Thank you for bringing me into this world and creating a leading edge for me with your brilliance. I'm grateful to have you as my mom.

Jenn- Thank you for being an amazing mother figure in my life. Your love and support has impacted me more than you may realize, I love you.

Gianna- I love you twinny. Life is so special with you. You are brilliant and I'm so grateful to have you in my life. Always have been and always will be.

Bella- You are a special woman to this world and I'm so lucky to see who you are, who you've become, and who you will continue to be. Thank you for being an amazing big sister and for all you've supported me in and through.

Ala - I love you. Thank you for cheering me on. Thank you for the ways you helped me grow into who I am. You have been such a powerful example of a woman and mother in my life. I admire you and appreciate who you are and who've you been in my life

Esther Hicks- Your work found me at the perfect time in my life and served as the launch pad for me to open to and create an incredible and meaningful life. Words can't express my gratitude for your work. THANK YOU!

Private and Sexy Wealthy Bitch Mastermind clients- You are the most incredible humans I have the pleasure of working with. Your dedication to your growth and impact blows my mind. I love your hearts. I love watching you grow. You are changing the world and I'm so proud to mentor you and do life with you.

Tyler and team- thank you for helping me bring this book into the world

Audrey, Sam, Jacquelynne- Thank you for the continual support you offer me. I couldn't do this without you. I'm grateful. I love you!

Mentors- Amanda, Melanie, Steph, Amy. Thank you for being in my world and always reminding me of who the fuck I am. Love you.

To everyone else who's supported me, expanded me, cheered me on with or without me knowing.. I'm grateful for you and I love you.

ABOUT THE AUTHOR

 Genevieve Rackham is a leading voice on wealth embodiment and getting rich. She has built a 7 figure business from the ground up focused on serving people who desire to have a sexy relationship with money. She brings a flare of play, ease, and a dash of sexy to getting rich and running and growing soul aligned businesses.

Genevieve mentors people all over the world who run 6, multiple 6, and 7 figure empires.

She has helped people all over the world ditch scarcity, get rich, and do it while feeling sexy. She believes more is always available to you, life gets to be good, and the universe wants you to be rich.

Her jam is money, growing your business, alignment, and letting it be sexy.

Photo taken by- www.themallorypaige.com

Made in the USA
Las Vegas, NV
11 November 2021

34245439R00070